MONSTERS

Sea Monsters

by Aaron Sautter

Reading Consultant:
Barbara J. Fox
Reading Specialist
North Carolina State University

Content Consultant:
David D. Gilmore
Professor of Anthropology
Stony Brook University
Stony Brook, New York

Capstone
press

Mankato, Minnesota

Blazers is published by Capstone Press,
151 Good Counsel Drive, P.O. Box 669, Mankato, Minnesota 56002.
www.capstonepress.com

Library of Congress Cataloging-in-Publication Data
Sautter, Aaron.
    Sea monsters / by Aaron Sautter.
    p. cm. —(Blazers. Monsters)
    Includes bibliographical references and index.
    ISBN-13: 978-0-7368-6442-8 (hardcover)
    ISBN-10: 0-7368-6442-3 (hardcover)
    1. Marine animals—Juvenile literature. 2. Sea monsters—Juvenile literature.
I. Title. II. Series.
QL122.2.S27 2007
001.944—dc22   2006001226

Summary: A brief explanation of legendary sea monsters, including their
development through history and their use in popular culture.

Editorial Credits
Jennifer Besel, editor; Juliette Peters, designer; Kelly Garvin, photo
    researcher/photo editor

Photo Credits
Capstone Press/Karon Dubke, cover, 4–5, 6–7, 7, 8–9
Corbis/Bettmann, 10–11, 26; Reuters, 18
Fortean Picture Library, 14, 17, 21, 22, 23; Robert Le Serrec, 28
Getty Images Inc./Universal Pictures, 27
The Granger Collection, New York, 25
Mary Evans Picture Library, 12, 13, 15, 24

1 2 3 4 5 6 11 10 09 08 07 06

Table of Contents

Danger at the Lake

On a cool, misty morning, two friends go fishing at the lake. They don't know the danger lurking in the water.

In the distance, they hear a splash. They look to see what made the noise. But they don't see the monster moving toward them.

Suddenly, the creature rises from the water behind them. Terrified, they turn and run for their lives.

Oceans Full of Monsters

The world's oceans and lakes are said to be full of legendary creatures. Sailors have told stories about sea monsters for thousands of years.

Some of the oldest sailor stories were about mermaids. Mermaids are beautiful women from the waist up. Below the waist, they flap powerful fish tails.

BLAZER FACT

Long ago, sailors believed
a mermaid's song could
make them jump off their
ship and drown.

Sailors also told tales of huge sea serpents in the ocean. They believed these monsters had flat heads and long, thick bodies.

The scariest stories were about the Kraken. Legends say the Kraken was bigger than a whale. It could crush a ship with just one of its huge tentacles.

BLAZER FACT

Some sailors thought the Kraken was as big as an entire island!

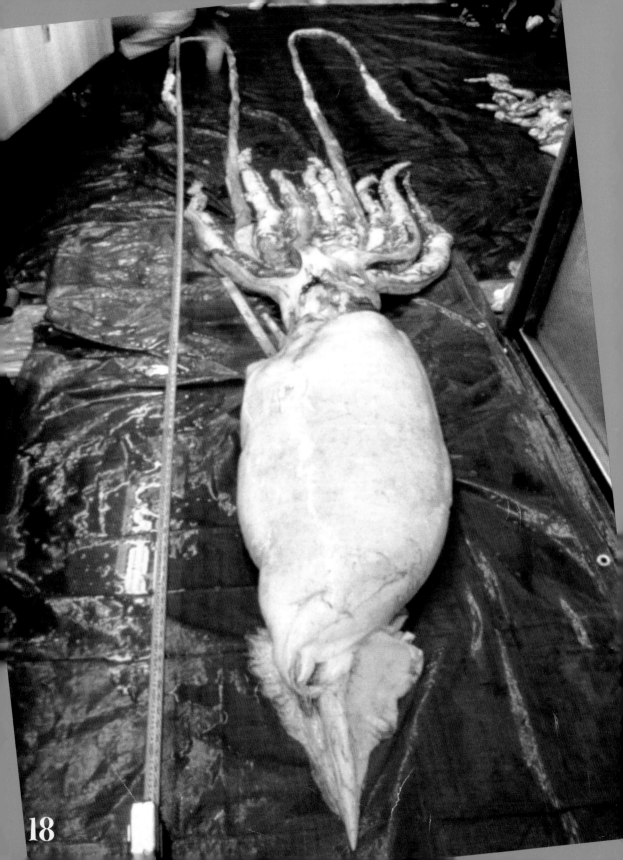

18

Stories about the Kraken may be based on a real animal. The giant squid grows to about 60 feet (18 meters) long. Sailors might have thought giant squids were monsters.

The legend of the Loch Ness Monster is the most famous sea monster story. Some people claim to have seen this large creature in a lake in Scotland.

BLAZER FACT

Other legends say there are monsters in lakes in New York and Canada.

Some people think this is a photograph of the mysterious Loch Ness Monster. Others think it's a fake photo.

In 1901, a long sea animal was caught in California. Today, many scientists think it was an oarfish.

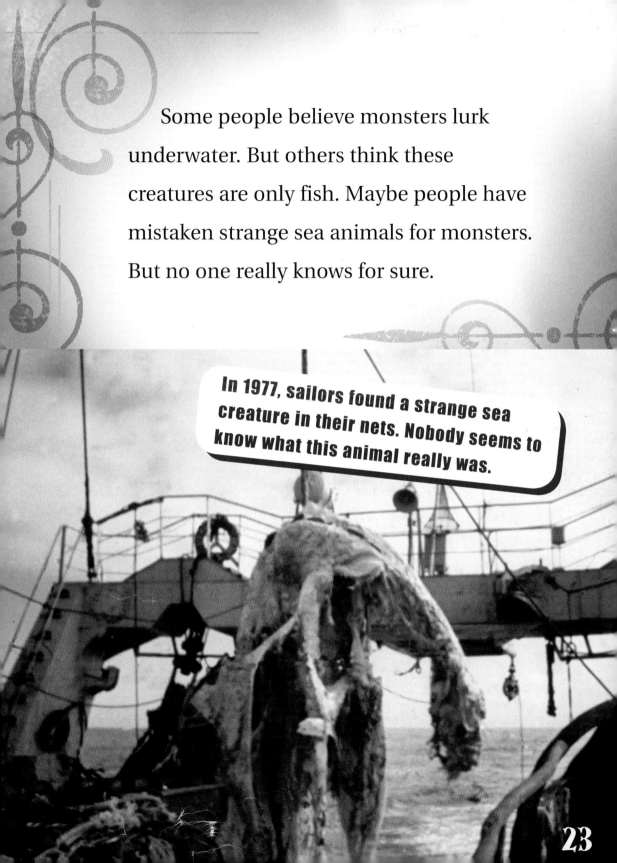

Some people believe monsters lurk underwater. But others think these creatures are only fish. Maybe people have mistaken strange sea animals for monsters. But no one really knows for sure.

In 1977, sailors found a strange sea creature in their nets. Nobody seems to know what this animal really was.

Finding Sea Monsters Today

Sea monster stories are fun and interesting. Many books have been written about creatures of the deep.

Some stories about sea monsters were so popular, they were made into movies.

There are many scary sea monster movies. In the 1950s, the Gill Man slithered into fame as a popular movie monster. Jaws, a huge shark, terrified people in the 1970s.

What lies deep below the water is still a mystery. Sea monster stories are strange and creepy. But are they real? What do you think?

Glossary

legendary (LEJ-uhnd-air-ee)—coming from a story handed down from earlier times

lurk (LURK)—to lie hidden, especially for an evil purpose

mysterious (miss-TIHR-ee-uhss)—hard to explain or understand

serpent (SUR-puhnt)—a snake

slither (SLITH-ur)—to slide along like a snake

tentacle (TEN-tuh-kuhl)—a long, flexible arm of an animal

MONSTERS

Read More

Cosson, M. J. *Sea Monsters: Myth and Truth.* Cover-to-Cover Books. Logan, Iowa: Perfection Learning, 2000.

Jay, Michael. *Sea Monsters.* Prehistoric Animals. Chicago: Raintree, 2004.

Sievert, Terri. *The Loch Ness Monster.* The Unexplained. Mankato, Minn.: Capstone Press, 2005.

Internet Sites

FactHound offers a safe, fun way to find Internet sites related to this book. All of the sites on FactHound have been researched by our staff.

Here's how:

1. Visit *www.facthound.com*

2. Choose your grade level.

3. Type in this book ID **0736864423** for age-appropriate sites. You may also browse subjects by clicking on letters, or by clicking on pictures and words.

4. Click on the **Fetch It** button.

FactHound will fetch the best sites for you!

Index